DINOSAUR WORLD

Long-Neck

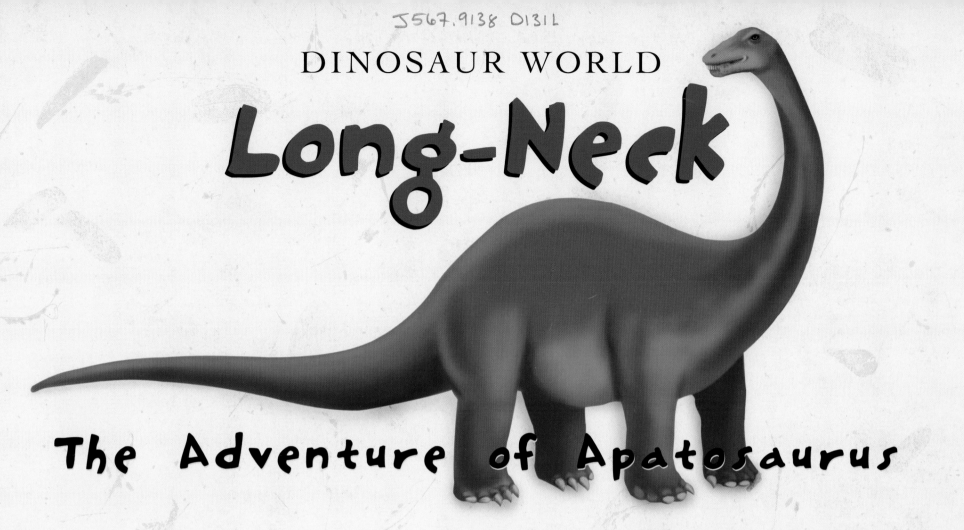

The Adventure of Apatosaurus

Written by Michael Dahl

Illustrated by Jeff Yesh

Thanks to our advisers for their expertise, research, knowledge, and advice:

Brent H. Breithaupt, Director
Geological Museum, University of Wyoming
Laramie, Wyoming

Peter Dodson, Ph.D.
Professor of Earth and Environmental Sciences
University of Pennsylvania
Philadelphia, Pennsylvania

Susan Kesselring, M.A.
Literacy Educator
Rosemount-Apple Valley-Eagan (Minnesota) School District

PICTURE WINDOW BOOKS
Minneapolis, Minnesota

Managing Editor: Bob Temple
Creative Director: Terri Foley
Editors: Nadia Higgins, Brenda Haugen
Editorial Adviser: Andrea Cascardi
Copy Editor: Laurie Kahn
Designer: Nathan Gassman
Page production: Picture Window Books
The illustrations in this book were rendered digitally.

Picture Window Books
5115 Excelsior Boulevard
Suite 232
Minneapolis, MN 55416
1-877-845-8392
www.picturewindowbooks.com

Printed in the United States of America.

Library of Congress Cataloging-in-Publication Data
Dahl, Michael.
Long-neck : the adventure of apatosaurus / written by Michael Dahl ;
illustrated by Jeff Yesh.
p. cm. — (Dinosaur world)
Summary: Explains how scientists learn about dinosaurs
and what their discoveries have revealed about Apatosaurus.
Includes bibliographical references and index.
ISBN 1-4048-0134-0
1. Apatosaurus Juvenile literature. [1. Apatosaurus. 2. Dinosaurs.]
I. Yesh, Jeff, 1971- ill. II. Title.
QE862.S3 D32 2004
567.913'8—dc21
                                        2003004162

No humans lived during the time of the dinosaurs. No people heard them roar, saw their scales, or felt their feathers.

The giant creatures are gone, but their fossils, or remains, lie hidden in the earth. Dinosaur skulls, skeletons, and eggs have been buried in rock for millions of years.

All around the world, scientists dig up fossils and carefully study them. Bones show how tall the dinosaurs stood. Claws and teeth show how they grabbed and what they ate. Scientists compare fossils with the bodies of living creatures such as birds and reptiles, who are relatives of the dinosaurs. Every year, scientists learn more and more about the giants that have disappeared.

Studying fossils and figuring out how the dinosaurs lived is like putting together the pieces of a puzzle that is millions of years old.

This is what some of those pieces can tell us about the dinosaur known as Apatosaurus.

The ground shook, and tall trees swayed. A female Apatosaurus (uh-PAT-uh-SAWR-us) thudded through a forest of ferns. Her feet dug into the soft earth, making footprints as wide as giant tire tracks.

Leaving the forest, she stopped. Her mighty foot scooped out a shallow hole in the sand. Apatosaurus stood over the hole and laid soft round eggs, one by one.

The longest trail of dinosaur footprints ever found in North America may have been left by Apatosaurus. Scientists discovered the tracks in the rocks of Colorado. The tracks traveled for a distance of 705 feet (215 meters).

The eggs were as big as soccer balls.
Some of the eggs dropped into the shallow nest
dug out by the mother Apatosaurus.
She covered the eggs with sand
to keep them safe until they hatched.

Apatosaurus was so huge that even when she squatted to lay eggs, the creature's bottom was still 8 feet (2½ meters) off the ground. Some of the eggs landed directly below the mother. Other eggs may have broken or rolled away.

Other eggs rolled away and landed in Apatosaurus's giant footprints. They were snatched up by hungry meat-eating dinosaurs.

One egg rolled along the ground until it stopped under a clump of soft ferns. The hidden egg grew hard. Soon the baby Apatosaurus was ready to hatch. The shell easily cracked open.

The young Apatosaurus spent most of her day eating berries, seeds, and ferns. Every day the creature ate 1 pound (½ kilogram) of food. By the end of her first year, she may have tripled in size.

The baby Apatosaurus crawled out of her shell.
She sniffed the air. Her huge eyes followed
the fluttering flight of busy moths.

The baby Apatosaurus grew into one of the largest creatures
that ever walked on land. She was longer than a tennis court.
Her body was taller than a modern-day elephant.

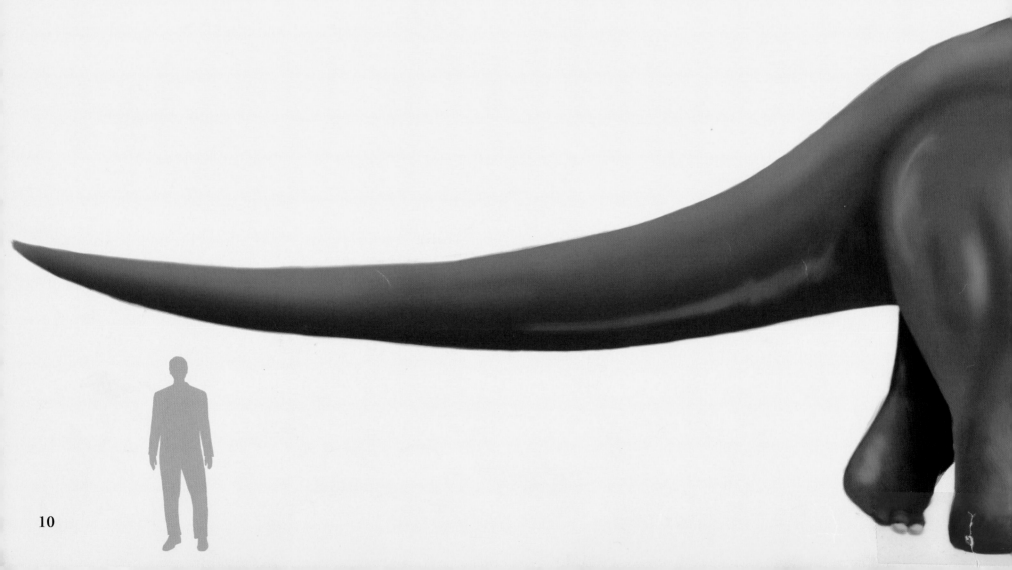

Apatosaurus's neck was as long as 20 feet (6 meters).
In fact, one nickname for this dinosaur is Long-Neck.

Apatosaurus could weigh as much as five
elephants. But her neck bones were hollow
and light, making her long neck easy to
move up and down.

The long neck of Apatosaurus was helpful for gathering food.

Apatosaurus's bulky body was too big to fit between the trees of a forest. She stood outside and stuck her long neck between the tree trunks. She nibbled on the soft plants on the forest floor.

Apatosaurus could lift her tiny head as high as a second-story window.

13

Apatosaurus had long, skinny teeth shaped like pencils.
The teeth pulled up plants but could not grind them.

So Apatosaurus also swallowed small pebbles.
The pebbles helped grind the food in the dinosaur's stomach.

If Apatosaurus could not reach the leafy top of a tree, she may have used her massive body to knock the tree down.

15

When Apatosaurus fed, she listened for the meat-eating dinosaur called Allosaurus (al-uh-SAWR-us). Allosaurus always was ready to attack Apatosaurus.

The bodies of the two enemies were almost the same height.
But Apatosaurus's long neck could lift her tiny head safely above
Allosaurus's deadly claws.

Sometimes the meat-eater won.
Scientists have found Apatosaurus
bones with teeth marks made
by a hungry Allosaurus.

17

Apatosaurus had other ways to defend herself. Her giant feet had thick, sharp claws.

Apatosaurus's amazing tail could stretch across a four-lane highway. An angry whip from this strong weapon could break another dinosaur's bones.

19

Less than 20 years after she crawled out of her egg,
Apatosaurus was ready to become a mother herself.

She mated with a male Apatosaurus who fed beside her.
Many months later, mother Apatosaurus laid dozens of eggs.

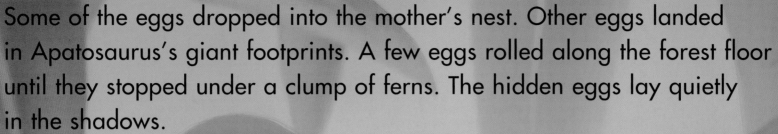

Some of the eggs dropped into the mother's nest. Other eggs landed in Apatosaurus's giant footprints. A few eggs rolled along the forest floor until they stopped under a clump of ferns. The hidden eggs lay quietly in the shadows.

Soon the shells began to crack open.

21

Apatosaurus: Where ...

In the United States, Apatosaurus fossils have been found in Colorado, Oklahoma, Utah, and Wyoming.

... and When

The "Age of Dinosaurs" began 248 million years ago (mya). If we imagine the time from the beginning of the dinosaur age to the present as one day, dinosaurs lived almost 18 hours — and humans appeared just 10 minutes ago!

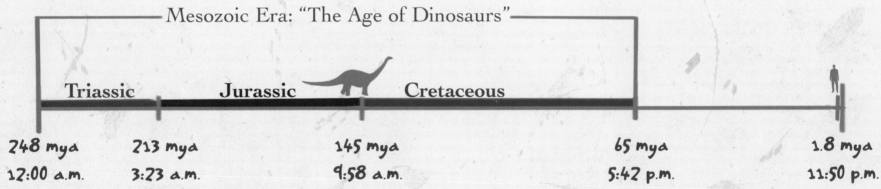

Mesozoic Era: "The Age of Dinosaurs"

Triassic   Jurassic   Cretaceous

248 mya	213 mya	145 mya	65 mya	1.8 mya
12:00 a.m.	3:23 a.m.	9:58 a.m.	5:42 p.m.	11:50 p.m.

Triassic—Dinosaurs first appear. Early mammals appear.
Jurassic—First birds appear.
Cretaceous—Flowering plants appear. By the end of this era, all dinosaurs disappear.

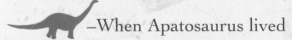—When Apatosaurus lived

—First humans appear

Digging Deeper

All About Eggs

No Apatosaurus eggs have ever been discovered. But Apatosaurus belonged to a family of dinosaurs called sauropods, whose eggs have been found. Titanosaurus (tie-TAN-uh-SAWR-uhs), a cousin to Apatosaurus, laid eggs in shallow nests scraped in the ground. It is a safe guess that Apatosaurus laid eggs as well. Some experts think Apatosaurus had a special egg-laying tube that grew out of her body. Other scientists think Apatosaurus dropped her eggs on the ground as she walked along, not bothering to stop and care for them.

Stiff Tail

Apatosaurus had powerful tail and leg muscles. Some scientists believe Apatosaurus could lean back and balance on its tail. This way the dinosaur could stand on its hind legs and reach leaves on very tall trees.

Lots of Birthdays

Apatosaurus may have lived for more than 100 years.

Heavy Meal

Apatosaurus would eat all day long, far into the night. Its daily diet of plant food may have weighed as much as 4,000 cheeseburgers!

Gone!

Apatosaurus disappeared from the earth about 140 million years ago. No one knows why.

Words to Know

dinosaur—a land reptile that lived in prehistoric times. All dinosaurs died out millions of years ago.
fern—a leafy, flowerless plant
fossil—the remains of a plant or animal that lived between thousands and millions of years ago
hatch—to break out of an egg

To Learn More

At the Library

Cohen, Daniel. *Apatosaurus*. Mankato, Minn.: Bridgestone, 2001.
Landau, Elaine. *Apatosaurus*. New York: Children's Press, 1999.
Willis, Dr. Paul. *Dinosaurs: My First Pocket Guide*. Washington, D.C: National
    Geographic Society, 1996.

On the Web

Enchanted Learning: Zoom Dinosaurs
http://www.EnchantedLearning.com/subjects/dinosaurs
For information, games, and jokes about dinosaurs, fossils, and prehistoric life

The Natural History Museum, London: Dino Directory
http://flood.nhm.ac.uk/cgi-bin/dino
For an alphabetical database of information on the Age of Dinosaurs

Fact Hound
Fact Hound offers a safe, fun way to find Web sites related to this book.
All of the sites on Fact Hound have been researched by our staff.
http://www.facthound.com

1. Visit the Fact Hound home page.
2. Enter a search word related to this book,
    or type in this special code: 1404801340.
3. Click on the FETCH IT button.

Your trusty Fact Hound will fetch the best sites for you!